Bread and Cup

for Elders at the
Communion Table

© 1976 by The Bethany Press

Cover art by Joan Fredman

Library of Congress Cataloging in Publication Data
Harrison, Russell F.   1918-
     Brief Prayers for Bread and Cup

     1. Lord's Supper—Prayer-books and devotions En-
glish, I. Title.
BV826.5.H37   265'.3   76-18932

ISBN: 0-8272-0211-3

Manufactured in the U.S.A.

Brief Prayers for Bread and Cup

For Elders at the Communion Table

Russell F. Harrison

The Bethany Press

SAINT LOUIS MISSOURI

Introduction

The Lord's table and the service of communion is central to the worship of Christians. The role of elders as they preside at the communion table is of far reaching significance.

Why this book? To encourage elders in brief communion prayer that leads those who worship into their own quiet moment of meditation and prayer.

Prayers by elders for the bread and for the cup should be looked upon as the beginning of continuing prayer on the part of each one who gathers to worship at the Lord's table. The elder leads them into prayer.

The three- and four-sentence prayer suggestions are intended to encourage the elder in brief but meaningful *introduction into prayer* as a central purpose when presiding at the communion table.

Such prayers for bread and cup should motivate and lead each worshiper into a personal, individual continuation of private, silent prayer throughout the service of communion.

Should these suggested prayers prove helpful to elders, then this little book will have achieved its intended purpose.

Russell F. Harrison

An Elder's Prayer of Commitment

Eternal God, I am grateful for the responsibility given me, as an elder, to be a part of worship at the Lord's table. Help me as I prepare for this service when I am asked to lead in prayer for bread or cup.

Grant that my voice may reflect reverence and confidence that others might find deeper meaning in these important moments for their lives.

Help me, O God, to speak clearly and distinctly, so that none may lose the meaning of the prayer offered for bread or cup.

Let me not forget the purpose of my communion prayer. May it first and foremost be a prayer to you as giver and sustainer of life. Grant that the words I use may be an outpouring of my own spirit, that I might come more fully into your presence and partake of your spirit.

In my prayer, O God, grant that I might be mindful of many others, coming as they do from so many backgrounds and experiences. There will be those who come to the communion table with burdens not shared by others who worship beside them. For some, this particular day will be a day of great joy. For others, sorrow may be deep upon their hearts. For the many, their lives will be as open vessels, waiting for some word in prayer which

I might say which will lead them along the pathway to fuller self-realization brought only by your abiding presence and inner spirit.

Keep me humble in the fulfilling of my task. Grant the assurance that my prayers at communion time will set the tone, help point the direction, and bring a creative dimension to what is thought, said, and done as once again we celebrate the supper of our Lord, in whose name we pray. Amen.

Suggested Prayers for
63 Sundays

• 1 •

Eternal God, guide our thoughts in individual prayer as we eat the bread. May each one of us recall the upper room and the eternal presence of Jesus, your son, which was promised to all who seek and follow him. Amen.

Our loving Father, in these moments of communion, we drink together the cup, remembering once again the sacrifice it represents. Forgive us our sins and shortcomings of this past week. Renew within each one of us the will to follow in your way. Amen.

Most merciful God, for these weekly moments of communion and meditation we are grateful. As we break the bread and eat together, may the presence of Christ become more real to each one of us. Help our individual and personal prayers to reflect our commitment and dedication. Amen.

As we take this cup in our hands, O God, may the spirit and presence of Jesus, our Lord, become more real for each one of us. May our prayers in silence, be those of gratitude, forgiveness, petition and rededication as we look to another week which lies before us. Amen.

Most gracious and eternal God, we give thanks for the gift of your son, Jesus, and for the Lord's supper which he gave to all generations in that upper room. Although we may be unworthy, the bread is given to us that our faith and strength might be renewed in worship each Sunday. May our quiet moments in prayer reflect our dedication. Amen.

Eternal God, bless the cup which we receive which symbolizes not only the sacrifice of Jesus your son, but reminds us of his abiding presence. As we drink of the cup, may it be with the assurance of your love for us that knows no bounds and has no end. In silent prayer we declare our gratitude and commitment. Amen.

As we receive the bread, our Father, may it be with our individual prayers of forgiveness. Our lives often reflect less than our best. We are grateful for these communion moments of reflection and pray they might guide us once again into a closer relationship to our Maker who sustains us each and every day. Amen.

Grant us, O God, the heart, mind and spirit to sense the deeper meanings of these moments of worship as we receive the cup. Our prayers are different because no two lives that you have created are the same. In quietness may be find hope, confidence and courage as we look to the coming week which lies before us. Amen.

• 5 •

Most loving Father, bless the loaf which represents to us the bread of life. We give thanks for the unnumbered blessings of this past week. Without our knowing you have given us much for which to be grateful. From the inner strength of these quiet moments, may we discover the deeper meanings of what it means to be Christian. Amen.

As we hold in our hands the cup, our Father, impress upon us the opportunity for newness of life. We come realizing that life is full and meaningful only when you are at the center of our being. Forgive us when we forget. As we pray silently, remind us once again. Amen.

We give praise, O God, for the good news of Jesus Christ and for these moments of communion and meditation. As we take the bread, may we remember not only the body broken for us, but the eternal presence of a living Christ. Hear each silent prayer in these quiet moments of reflection. Amen.

Bless the cup, O Lord, reminding us once again that we are bought with so great a price. Forgive us for opportunities missed for Christian witness this past week. Make us sensitive this coming week to daily opportunities for witnessing to your presence. Amen.

In joy and gratitude, we take this
bread, our Father. May we partake in a
spirit of thanksgiving. Grant that the
moments of silent prayer may bring
us to a deeper sense of your divine
presence in our lives. Bless us as we
prepare spiritually to begin another
week. Amen.

Our loving heavenly Father, we take
the cup, symbolic of Christ's suffering
for each one of us. As those attempting
to be his followers, we pray that in
these silent moments you will guide
our thoughts and prayers. Amen.

For bringing us to this table on the first day of another week, we give thanks, our Father. As we receive the bread may we be reminded of the great love with which you have blessed each one of us. Hear our individual prayers of thanksgiving, penitence and petition as we prepare to live and serve you this coming week. Amen.

Eternal God, bless the cup which we shall drink to remind us once again that Jesus, the Christ, died upon the cross that we might have life and have it abundantly. We are grateful for the victory of Easter over the darkness of Friday's crucifixion. In that hope of life eternal we drink the cup in Jesus' name. Amen.

God of the universe and all peoples
everywhere, we break and eat this
bread to symbolize once again our
recognition that life is your greatest
gift to each one of us. In quietness, and
in the solitude of each individual
prayer, hear us as we seek to know and
do your will this coming week. Amen.

Our Father, for thousands of groups
worshiping this day across the earth,
the bread we receive represents the life
giving presence of Christ. As we drink
of the cup, may we renew by our own
longings through prayer a closer walk
with him in whose name we have these
moments of communion meditation.
Amen.

• 10 •

Eternal God, bless the bread we eat this day as we acknowledge the living presence of our Lord and Savior, Jesus Christ. May his death on the cross and his victory over the tomb assure us of life eternal. Grant that our prayers of rededication in the silence of this communion may prepare us for another week. Amen.

Our loving Father, the cup symbolizes for us the sacrifice which has been made for us. As we partake help us to be mindful of the love which has brought us to this moment. Grant that the inspiration of these quiet moments in prayer may make us more receptive to your will for our daily lives. Amen.

• 11 •

As we partake of this bread, our
Father, may we be strengthened in our
commitment to Jesus Christ. Grant
that his presence may be felt as we
gather around this communion table
and bring before you as our God, the
innermost prayers of our hearts. Amen.

Eternal God, we receive this cup which
symbolizes for us the sacrifice of Jesus
upon the cross. We rejoice this day in
his victory which has given to each of
us the promise of life eternal. In our individual prayers we dedicate ourselves
anew to living our lives more fully in
loving service this coming week.
Amen.

We give thanks for the loaf, our Father, recognizing that it is the bread of life. In our moments of meditation, may our prayers find favor in your sight. Fill us with your eternal spirit as we worship in the quiet of this communion hour. Amen.

Most merciful Father, we are grateful for this house of worship where we might have the privilege of celebrating once again the Lord's supper. We give thanks for those across the ages who have helped keep alive your church that we may have this opportunity today. May each one in the silence of unspoken prayer find comfort, guidance, forgiveness and inspiration. Amen.

• 13 •

Eternal God, grant that the eating of
this bread might remind us once again
of your never failing love. As we gather
around this table of remembrance,
may your spirit fill us with renewed
desire to do your will. Bless our silent
prayers where each one takes these
moments to seek your presence and the
strength that comes in sensing that you
are near. Amen.

O God, we give thanks for the cup,
remembering that we are bought with
so great a price. As we drink together
of the wine, bless our kinship with all
Christians everywhere who turn to you
this day in prayer. May our quiet
moments of individual meditation be
moments of renewal for the week that
lies ahead. Amen.

• 14 •

Gracious Father, we partake of the bread at this communion hour, in full recognition of imperfection in each of our lives. As physical bread sustains life, may the spiritual bread we receive nourish and enrich our inner lives. Grant that our individual prayers may be pleasing in your sight. Amen.

Bless the cup, O God, which reminds us once again of the upper room where Jesus met with his disciples. We are grateful for what these quiet moments have meant across the years to each one of us. May our silent prayers this day bring a new sense of direction and assurance for the days ahead. Amen.

• 15 •

Our loving God, whose love has
brought us to this table to receive the
bread, we give our thanks. Forgive us
for our sins and shortcomings of the
past. In personal prayer, help each one
to find new directions for life this coming week. Amen.

Eternal God, we are awed, as we think
of the billions of people who across the
ages have taken this cup. In this high
moment of our worship this day,
deepen our kinship with this great
cloud of witnesses. Bless each prayer
this moment brings. Amen.

May these moments of communion lift up our prayers for forgiveness, as we partake of this bread, O God. May we find strength to begin another week, praying for a closer walk with you, the source of our being. Bless each silent prayer this day. Amen.

Our Father, we recall the twelve in an upper room, as Jesus took the cup and reminded his disciples that as often as they ate the bread and drank the cup, they should do so in remembrance of him. May our individual prayers seek your presence and your strength which we need for a fuller living of this coming week.

• 17 •

In joy we come to receive this bread, remembering all that has been done for us that we might come to this moment of communion. Grant us a fuller sense of the mission and witness to which we have been called. Renew each one in the moments of silence and meditation. Amen.

For the privilege of taking this communion cup, at the beginning of a new week, we express our deep gratitude, O God. Be with us as we seek a fuller understanding of your will for each one gathered here. Help us to pray not only for ourselves but for one another. Amen.

Most gracious God, as we eat of this bread, make us mindful of the gift of life. As we come to this communion table, may our gratitude take the form of new commitment. Bless each silent prayer of renewal and dedication in these moments of meditation. Amen.

Eternal God, the cup represents to us the sacrifice of Jesus upon the cross which gives assurance of life eternal. For the Easter victory, the foundation of our Christian hope, we give our thanks. Teach us to pray in our quiet unspoken thoughts that we might sense the assurance of your abiding presence. Amen.

Bless, O God, the bread as Jesus blessed it in the upper room. As we eat may we recognize the presence symbolized by our reliving together that experience of the upper room today. In our silent prayer at this communion hour grant us direction for living this coming week. Amen.

The cup which we hold in our hand, reminds us, O God, that we have been bought with a price. For each one, may the drinking of it, bring forgiveness, gratitude, assurance and hope. Amen.

We give thanks, our Father, for the bread of life, which we share each Lord's day at this communion hour. Grant that all our prayers may be acceptable in your sight. Bless each one in this time of quiet meditation and rededication. Amen.

As we drink of the cup, O God, may its symbolism fill our minds and hearts with a deeper grasp of our Christian faith. In our individual prayers, guide us that we may discover new truth and direction because you are near. Amen.

Most merciful God, for the privilege of
seeing the dawning of this another
day, we express our heartfelt thanks. In
appreciation of all that you have done
for us, we take this bread and rededicate ourselves to the tasks of witness
and service. May each one in the silence
of unspoken prayer seek the guidance
needed for living more fully this coming week. Amen.

Eternal Father of all peoples everywhere, we are grateful for the universal Christian faith of which we are
a part. May the drinking of this cup remind us of the responsibilities which
accompany such a great privilege.
Bless each prayer of this communion
hour. Amen.

Our loving God, whose son laid down his life upon a cross that we might receive eternal life, we give thanks for this bread. At the Lord's table receive our silent and our spoken prayers that our lives might become more acceptable in your sight. Amen.

Our Father, we recall the upper room where Jesus took the cup and instituted this service of communion which Christians might receive for all time to come. We are glad to be a part of so great a fellowship. Bless our prayers offered silently now around this table of remembrance. Amen.

• 23 •

Gracious God, for the beauty of life and the opportunity for prayerful reflection, accept our thanks. Each week as we receive the bread and break it together the opportunity is ours to receive in the silence of our own thoughts and prayers your presence and guidance. Help us all to live more fully each day of the coming week because of what happens here. Amen.

Bless to our comfort and strength this cup which symbolizes to us, O God, the upper room. May our quiet prayer bring us closer to you now. Amen.

Our Father, we give thanks for the bread which makes us one with all Christians everywhere. On the first day of another week we come to the Lord's table to seek strength and guidance for the days which lie ahead. Bless each silent prayer of this communion time. Amen.

We accept this cup, O Lord, as a symbol of the great sacrifice which Jesus made upon the cross, that we might come to know the way, the truth and the life. Accept the prayers offered in quiet meditation here this day. Amen.

• 25 •

For the mystery of life itself, we give
our thanks, O God. As we take the
bread and eat of it together in this
communion hour, grant that we may
find direction and renewal. Hear the
individual prayers of mind and heart as
we come to this table. Amen.

Eternal God, as we drink the cup in
these moments of worship, we confess
our unworthiness. In the quiet times of
reflection, hear the prayers of those
who seek to follow more closely in your
pathway. Amen.

May the loaf we eat this day at the Lord's table, bring us into a deeper fellowship as the living church. Enable us to accept the responsibility of discipleship. In silent prayer, guide each thought in our seeking to find direction and purpose for our lives. Amen.

Grant that the receiving of the cup may remind us once again of your great love and the sacrifice of your son. May our silent moments of gratitude and petition bring to each one present the courage and direction for a fuller life this coming week. Amen.

With thanksgiving, O God, we share
together in the eating of this bread.
We are grateful for the love and
sacrifice it represents. May the spoken
and silent prayers of this communion
hour be acceptable in your sight.
Amen.

Most gracious God, as we drink the
cup, may we recall the first Lord's
supper. For this weekly reminder of
who we are, and with what a price we
have been bought, we are thankful.
Bless each prayer during these moments of commitment and rededication. Amen.

• 28 •

We are thankful, our Father, for the gift of life which enables us to see the beginning of another week. As we take the bread, may its meaning become more significant in each of our lives. Grant that the unspoken prayers may draw us closer to you. Amen.

Eternal God, we marvel at the wonders of your creation. The mystery of the communion service as we partake together of this cup, keeps us seeking a better way and a fuller life. Bless all of our prayers in these moments of communion meditation. Amen.

• 29 •

As we receive the bread, our Father, may our hearts and minds be open to the leading of your Holy Spirit. May our prayers in the secret of our innermost being be those of confidence and assurance. Amen.

Bless the cup, which represents once again to us a reminder of the great love you have for each one of us. May our prayers be those of gratitude for the gift of your son. Amen.

As we partake of the bread, O God, sharpen our awareness and appreciation of the beauty around us. Help us to use wisely all that you have given us, to your glory. Bless each personal prayer of forgiveness, petition and guidance for the days ahead. Amen.

As we hold in our hand the cup, our Father, may your spirit renew a right spirit within us. As we drink together, bring to each heart and mind those prayers in these quiet moments which bring commitment, renewal and assurance. Amen.

Eternal God, remind us that we are
part of so great a cloud of witnesses,
when we receive the bread in this service of communion. May our prayers
be those of gratitude and commitment.
Amen.

Almighty God, we are grateful for the
Lord's supper and the partaking of the
cup. As we drink together in these
moments of communion, bless each
silent and spoken prayer, that all might
find renewal for the living of this coming week. Amen.

Our Father, we give thanks for the church of Jesus Christ across the world today. In fellowship with peoples everywhere we break bread and seek strength and the will to serve. Grant that the silent moments may bring to each one present the opportunity for prayerful commitment. Amen.

Bless the cup, O Lord, that in the drinking of it together we might sense the presence of your Holy Spirit. May each prayer offered here this day, be pleasing in your sight. Amen.

We appreciate your loving kindness
toward us, O God, and receive this
bread as the bread of life. We
remember those who lived and died in
ages past that we might have this
observance of the Lord's supper here
today. Bless each prayer offered in love
and appreciation. Amen.

Eternal God, in the drinking of this
cup, strengthen our commitment.
Forgive us for falling short of your will
for each of our lives. May the moments
of silence which follow, be opportunity
for our individual prayers of renewal
and dedication. Amen.

Most merciful Father, the symbolic act of breaking bread together makes us one with all peoples everywhere who are part of the Christian fellowship. May the awareness of being in so great a company inspire us to better living. Grant that the silent prayers of this quiet moment may prepare us for the week ahead. Amen.

Our Father and our God, as we hold in our hands this cup, we express once again our thanks for your Son and his sacrifice upon the cross. May our silent prayers be those of forgiveness, petition, intercession for others, and gratitude for all that you have done for us. Amen.

As we receive the bread, the sustenance of life itself, O God, we remember the upper room and the spiritual values which Jesus placed upon the breaking of bread in the quiet of communion. Help us to find new meaning in an ancient custom, as we pray silently for ourselves, each other and all peoples everywhere. Amen.

For the eternal presence represented by this cup, we are grateful, our Father. May this hour of worship bring us into a closer sense of fellowship with you, our God. Bless each prayer offered in this moment of communion and meditation. Amen.

Eternal God, as we partake of the bread, grant each one of us a renewed sense of your presence. In the eating of the bread together we once again recall Jesus as he sat with his disciples in an upper room. May we identify with all who since that time have paused in silent and spoken prayer around the communion table. Amen.

O God, who has created us in your image, we acknowledge that many times we fall short of your will for our lives. As we take this cup, may our individual and personal prayers reflect our renewal and rededication. Amen.

• 37 •

Most gracious and eternal God, bless
the bread which we receive at this
communion hour. Grant that the inspiration of these moments of silent
prayer and meditation may open up to
each one of us a sense of direction and
hope. Amen.

Our loving Father, the cup reminds us
of the sacrifice of Jesus upon the cross.
Unworthy though we may be, we are
grateful for your many blessings. In
the quietness of this communion moment, may each prayer be acceptable
in your sight. Amen.

God of all peoples across the earth, we join with millions who in the act of breaking the bread acknowledge the lordship of Jesus in their personal lives. May each prayer here in this sanctuary at the Lord's table of communion be the longing for a closer walk and a more dedicated life in Jesus' name. Amen.

Bless, our Father, the cup of sacrifice which binds us to Christians across the world and across the ages this day. Give us insight as we have this opportunity for silent prayer, that the coming week may find us more in tune with your will and purpose for our lives. Amen.

God of all creation, fill us with the joy
of this communion as we take again
the bread which feeds our spirits. We
celebrate the gift of Jesus whose presence here gives hope to all who name
him as Lord of life. Bless each silent
prayer as we partake together. Amen.

Eternal Father, we give thanks for the
cup. May it symbolize to us the opportunity to find anew our mission and
purpose as we live our days upon
the earth. Grant that each unspoken
prayer may be the seeking of a better
and fuller understanding of your will
for each one of us in the days of this
coming week. Amen.

In gratitude we gather about this communion table, O God, to receive the bread as followers and disciples of Jesus. Bless each silent unspoken prayer and help each one to find that sense of your love, forgiveness, and guidance now and in the days to come. Amen.

Most merciful and gracious God, accept our thanks for this cup. As we reflect, each in personal silent prayer, upon its deeper meaning for life, grant us a renewal of faith and commitment this day. Amen.

Our loving Father, we are remembering as we take the bread, your great love which brought the gift of your son. May these quiet moments of reflection and meditation help us find direction for the days and weeks ahead. Amen.

Everlasting God, as we gather about the Lord's table to receive this cup, we are mindful of the Easter victory over the darkness of Good Friday. Hear our individual silent prayers of gratitude and petition that we might be more receptive to your will and spirit as we face life and its opportunities for service. Amen.

Eternal God, for the privilege of being here around the communion table to partake together of the bread, we give our heartfelt thanks. In the solitude of silent prayer, may each one search deeply for your presence and sense the assurance of your guidance in the days ahead. Amen.

Our loving Father, our worship is made more meaningful as we recognize your universal presence as we receive this communion cup. We join with millions who this day pause to pray, each one silently in his or her own way. Bless us in our quiet moments of meditation. Amen.

As Jesus took the bread and blessed it, we take the loaf in gratitude and thanksgiving today. We come to this table not because we must but because we may. Guide us in our individual silent prayers that each one might know your love and your guiding presence. Amen.

God of all peoples everywhere, we are grateful to be part of your vast human family across the earth. May the drinking of this cup remind us of our responsibilities which are part of the privilege of being Christian in our day. Amen.

Most merciful God, we give thanks for this bread which was broken for us, first in an upper room and now today to remind us that we have been bought with a great price. Because of what happens here in these moments of reflection and meditation, may our lives be more open to those opportunities of service which may be ours this coming week. Amen.

Our Father, bless the cup which we receive today. As we drink of the fruit of the vine may our silent prayers be those of penitence, asking your forgiveness, and those of petition, asking your guidance in the days ahead. Amen.

• 45 •

Most gracious God, we come partaking
of the bread and seeking a renewed
sense of your presence. We are unworthy of the great love which has
been implanted within us. Yet, in
silent and spoken prayer we would
seek to find ways of sharing that great
love with others as we live this coming
week. Amen.

Bless the cup, our Father, which opens
for us anew the reality of our faith. We
are grateful that you have received us
into the fellowship of your church.
Bless our prayer moments of communion and meditation. Amen.

Eternal God, grant that this bread may be to us the bread of the spirit as we partake together at this communion hour. On the first day of another week, we pause to seek your guidance. Receive the spoken and silent prayers of each one as we seek strength and direction for the days ahead. Amen.

We give thanks for this cup, O God, remembering that our lives are imperfect and in need of your presence and help. Bless these quiet moments of reflection and may our lives be enriched for greater service. Amen.

• 47 •

As we receive the bread at the Lord's table, Our Father, grant that we may be open to the opportunity life provides for witness and service. Forgive us for missed opportunities and bless us in our silent and spoken prayer in these moments of communion. Amen.

Most gracious God, as we hold in our hands this cup, and drink of it in prayerful remembrance of Jesus and his death upon the cross, make us instruments for good in the world. We have fallen short of your expectation and ask your blessing as we turn to you in the quiet of these moments together. Amen.

Dear God, we think of the hungry across the earth today as we partake of this communion bread. Sharpen our sensitivity to human need whether at our own doorstep or in a distant land. We thank you for these moments of quiet where each one can seek your will and guidance. Amen.

Our Father, in humility we take this cup realizing that we are unworthy of all that for us has been so freely given. In the silence of this communion service, grant that each may seek a renewed commitment to living more fully the Christian faith. Amen.

Eternal God, for the daily bread that
sustains our bodies we are most
grateful. For the breaking of bread in a
spiritual sense at the Lord's table, we
are truly thankful. Hear the spoken
and unspoken prayers and use each
person here in greater fulfillment of
your mission. Amen.

As we hold the cup in our hands this
day, our Father, it is with remembrance of what it represents. Let us
remember the sacrifice of Jesus upon
the cross and the victory which assures
us, too, of eternal life. Bless each silent
prayer in these moments of dedication.
Amen.

• 50 •

Most merciful God, we give thanks that we are able to be here in your house of worship this morning for the breaking of bread. Bless those who for health or other reasons can not be present here today. Grant that each prayer in the quietness of this communion hour may bring each person into closer fellowship with you for guidance in the days ahead. Amen.

Most gracious God, bless now the cup, and the sacrifice it represents. Bless us in our seeking of your will in daily life as we turn to you in the silence of personal and individual prayer as we commune with one another and with you, our God. Amen.

• 51 •

Our everlasting God, for the promise
and assurance of the Christian faith we
express our thanks through the breaking of bread together this day. Grant
that each prayer in the moments of
meditation that are to follow might
open us anew to the leading of your
guiding spirit. Amen.

Most merciful Father, we give thanks
for the cup. As we drink of it, may we
find a new sense of mission as followers
of Jesus. Forgive us when we have
fallen short of what we are capable. In
our silent prayers during this communion service, grant that we may
sense renewal, insight and dedication.
Amen.

Eternal God, in a hungry world bread is the symbol of life. As we come to the Lord's table, may the breaking of bread symbolize for us partaking of spiritual bread to sustain our souls. We give thanks for Jesus and his sacrifice of life itself on our behalf. Strengthen our commitment and enlighten our understanding in the moments of quiet meditation during this service. Amen.

Almighty God, who has redeemed the world and all who dwell therein, we take the cup as an act of joining all of those who are working in the establishment of your Kingdom. Help us to do our part in bringing peace to a troubled world and peace to a troubled heart, as we may find or make opportunity. Bless our prayers of silent dedication. Amen.

• 53 •

Our Creator and our God, we marvel
at the wonder, mystery and beauty of
all creation. In appreciation for all that
you provide for us daily, we take this
bread and break it in an act of
rededication to the tasks of witness and
service. Guide us during this coming
week. Bless our silent prayers in this
moment of communion. Amen.

Bless, O God, to our comfort and
strength this fruit of the vine which
symbolizes for us the upper room. We
are grateful for the example which
Jesus has set before us. May our quiet
prayer bring us each one, and all
together, to a closer relationship with
you as our God. Amen.

We are always grateful, O Lord, for the dawning of each new day, and in the breaking of bread express our thanks. Guide the thoughts of our silent prayers that we may know how to pray. Bless us during this coming week. Amen.

We remember, our Father, how Jesus in the upper room, took the cup and gave it to his disciples asking that as often as they take the cup, they do so in remembrance of him. We now give our thanks and in moments of silent prayer commit ourselves to greater Christian service during the week to come. Amen.

Eternal God, and Father of all peoples
everywhere, we are grateful for the universal faith of which we are a part.
May the breaking of bread in this communion hour remind us of the responsibilities which accompany so great a
privilege. Bless our silent prayers this
day. Amen.

Our loving Father, whose son laid
down his life upon a cross that we
might receive eternal life, we give
thanks for this cup. At the Lord's table
we bring our silent and our spoken
prayers, asking that our lives might
become more acceptable in your sight.
Amen.

God creative, who abides with all who call upon you, enter the hearts and lives of those assembled here, as once again we break the bread which symbolizes once more the presence of Jesus among us. Bless each and every prayer which rises up in our innermost being and guide us during this coming week. Amen.

O God, whose truth we seek in these moments of communion and personal meditation, bless the cup which we receive this day. Turn our thoughts from that which would represent less than our best, to those creative yearnings which will bring us close to you. May our prayers be acceptable in your sight. Amen.

God of stability, in a world of confusion and instability, we are grateful that we may come together in this house of worship to break bread in your Son's name. From many differing experiences this past week, we come quietly, to seek your presence and a sense of your guiding spirit. In silent prayer may each one find new commitment to the way, the truth and the life. Amen.

Most patient God, we know how many times we fall short of your will for our lives. In the taking of this cup today, may our minds and hearts find anew the comfort and strength which only you can give to those who turn to you in prayer. Bless each inner prayer as we seek your guidance for our living of the week ahead. Amen.

Blessed God, whose mercy is never failing, we are grateful for your abiding presence. As we break the bread in this communion hour, bless each and every prayer. Give us the courage for living a Christian life. Grant us the wisdom of decision when life's choices come to bear upon us. Bless us this coming week. Amen.

O God, who reaches out to all who seek you, and who waits patiently for our return when we forget or forsake you, bless now this cup of the Lord's supper as we partake of it. May our prayers bring to a sharper focus the longings of our minds and hearts. Bless each prayer offered to you during this communion hour. Amen.

• 59 •

O God, whose loving kindness knows
no end, we break the bread acknowl-
edging the continuing presence of
Jesus, your son. Forgive us for those
missed opportunities this past week
which would have made us better than
we are. Bless each silent prayer in
these moments of communion as we
observe once again the Lord's supper.
Amen.

Eternal Creator, in thanksgiving we
take in our hands the cup this day,
mindful of who we are and what we
are meant to be. Grant that our prayers
may be pleasing in your sight. Help
our silent longings be those of deeper
dedication and commitment as we face
a whole new week that lies ahead.
Amen.

God of justice, wisdom and truth, accept our prayers this day as we take the bread, break it and are reminded once again of the great price given for us. Grant us a new sense of responsibility for being the church in your world in our time. Bless each prayer, both silent and unspoken, here today. Amen.

Most gracious God, who never forsakes us, even in our weakest moments, we give thanks for the cup. In the assurance of your love and forgiveness we drink this cup, praying each one present, that our lives might be used more fully in your service during the week ahead. Amen.

For your abiding presence, O God, we are thankful. Unworthy though we might be, your love still surrounds and sustains us. Help us to be instruments of your love and concern as we receive the bread and break it together in this communion hour. Bless each and every prayer and guide us all into a fuller relationship with you, as our God. Amen.

Ever present God, hear our prayers this day as we rededicate ourselves. We would remember peoples in our own community and around the world not nearly as richly blessed as are we. Grant that in our silent prayers we may commit ourselves to greater daily service, in your name. Amen.

Almighty God, whose presence is ever near to those who turn to you in prayer, bless now the bread as we partake of the Lord's supper together. May our silent and spoken prayers be those of gratitude. Grant that in these moments we may find strength, hope and direction for another week. Amen.

We take the cup, O God, signifying the presence of Jesus, and seek as did the disciples in that upper room, your will for our lives. In our human frailty, we know how easy it is for us to stray from the path that you would have us follow. In quietness may we, each one, dedicate ourselves anew to your service. Amen.

God of eternal love, as the daily bread sustains our physical bodies, may the breaking of spiritual bread sustain our eternal being. We are grateful for Jesus who set before us the way, the truth and the life. Guide us in praying those silent, unspoken prayers that will lead us forward in the days to come. Amen.

God of both time and eternity, we take this cup, symbolic of the sacrifice Jesus made upon the cross. We are grateful for the victory which was his and the promise which has come to each one of us. In our moments of individual prayer, may we find assurance, hope, confidence and renewed commitment. Amen.

Communion

	Please Check		Write in Date
	Bread	Cup	
1			
2			
3			
4			
5			
6			
7			
8			
9			
10			
11			
12			
13			
14			
15			
16			
17			
18			

Prayer Record

	Please Check		Write in Date
19	Bread	Cup	
20			
21			
22			
23			
24			
25			
26			
27			
28			
29			
30			
31			
32			
33			
34			
35			
36			

Communion

	Please Check		Write in Date
	Bread	Cup	
37			
38			
39			
40			
41			
42			
43			
44			
45			
46			
47			
48			
49			
50			
51			
52			
53			
54			

Prayer Record

	Please Check		Write in Date
	Bread	Cup	
55			
56			
57			
58			
59			
60			
61			
62			
63